The Littlest Giant
The Story of Vamana

The Littlest Giant

The Story of Vamana

~ A MANDALA CHILDREN'S CLASSIC ~

Text by Joshua M. Greene

Illustrations by Emma V. Moore

INSIGHT KIDS
A MANDALA BOOK

San Rafael, California

Long ago when the world was young, there lived a king named Bali who wanted to be the greatest king of all. Bali's kingdom was already very big, but not big enough for him. He wanted more.

ali had no friends, but he did have a wicked adviser named Shukra.

"If you want to be greatest of all," Shukra told Bali, "you must do something great. Go and conquer the world."

Bali always did what Shukra told him to do.
He put on his mighty armor. He grabbed his
mighty bow. He mounted his mighty chariot
and off he went.

Bali did conquer the world, but afterwards he
was not happy, for his kingdom was still not
big enough.

"Well done," said Shukra. "But if you *really* want to be the greatest king of all, now you must conquer the galaxy."

As always, Bali did what Shukra told him to do. He once again put on his mighty armor. He grabbed his mighty bow and arrows, mounted his mighty chariot, and off he went.

ali conquered the galaxy. His kingdom extended far and wide, but still he was not happy. "What more must I do to be the greatest king of all?" he wondered. "What is left for me to conquer?"

Far away in the spiritual world,
Vishnu, the Supreme Person, watched.
He understood Bali's unhappiness
and came up with a plan.

eanwhile, Shukra had his own plan to make Bali greater. "Build a blazing fire," he told the king. "Chant magic spells. Conquer the entire universe and truly become the greatest king of all!"

Bali thought, "Shukra is my adviser. Surely I should do what he says." Bali built a blazing fire and chanted magic spells. The fire glowed brighter and brighter, and every being in the universe trembled.

Out from the flames stepped a beautiful little person, no bigger than a child. Bali was amazed. He rose from his throne and greeted his guest with polite words. He was very attracted to his glowing form.

"Greetings, little sir. May I offer you a place to sit? May I offer you something to eat? I have great wealth. Ask me for anything at all, and I will give it to you."

Shukra narrowed his eyes. There was something strange about this little person.

"**D**ear king," said the little person from the fire. "I do not need much, just a bit of land as wide as my three steps."

"Hah!" laughed Bali. "That is not enough. Ask me for something greater. I have elephants and villages. I have planets and stars. Ask for greater treasure, and I will give it to you."

"No need," said the little person. "The greatest treasures are often not very big. Think of a fruit or a flower. Think of a cup of fresh water or the company of friends. Real treasures can be very small, can they not? Do not be fooled by size. Small can also be great."

"Do not listen to him!" whispered Shukra. "I suspect this is Vishnu, the Supreme Person. He will cheat you and take everything. Then where will we be?"

Bali waved him away. He liked his little guest. For the first time, Bali refused to do what Shukra told him to do.

"Little sir," Bali said. "You may have your wish."

"I curse you for disobeying me!" Shukra yelled at Bali. "Now we will lose everything." And off he went, grumbling about how much a little person can do.

"Take your three steps," Bali said.

hen the little person started to grow. He grew and he grew,
until he was a giant and his head touched the clouds.
People gasped and animals ran, but the giant continued to grow.

He lifted one foot and stepped so wide he covered the Earth.

he giant grew more and more, until no one could see where he began or where he ended. He lifted his other foot, and his next step covered the planets.

The giant's toe pierced the covering of the universe and down
fell a stream of water. Today, it is known as the River Ganges.
On the giant's foot, Bali saw a lotus flower, an umbrella, a chariot,
a fish, and a peacock fan. Who but the Supreme Person would have
such beautiful designs on his feet?

"Shukra was right," Bali thought. "This is the Supreme Person Vishnu.
And He *has* indeed taken everything. Now what shall I do?"

The giant looked down on Bali. "I am the Supreme Vishnu," he said, "Lord of all the worlds. In the form you see before you, I am called Vamana. And you, O king, have taken what does not belong to you. That is not great. That is greed, which can never be satisfied.

"You promised me three steps," Vamana said, "but there is no place left. Where shall I put my third step?"

ali folded his hands together and his eyes filled with tears. "I have indeed been greedy," he said. "But I would like you to be my friend. That would mean more to me than having the greatest of kingdoms."

Bali fell to his knees. "Please put your third step here, on my head."

Vamana grew smaller and smaller, until he was again a little person. Then he lifted his foot and placed it on Bali's head. After that, Bali returned all that he had conquered.

Vamana was pleased by Bali's sincerity and gave him back his kingdom. For his part, Bali had understood a valuable lesson.

Sometimes, the biggest treasures come in packages that are very, very small.

A Note to Parents and Teachers

The Littlest Giant is a retelling of the original story found in the Bhagavata Purana, a revered Sanskrit text. Vamana is one of the avatars or incarnations of Vishnu, the Supreme Being. Each avatar brings wisdom into the world for the guidance of humanity. For young readers, few heroic figures from India are as beloved as Vamana, the littlest giant.

INSIGHT KIDS
A MANDALA BOOK

PO Box 3088
San Rafael, CA 94912
www.insighteditions.com

Text copyright © 2014 Joshua M. Greene
Illustrations copyright © 2014 Emma V. Moore
Design by Malea Clark-Nicholson

Cataloging-in-Publication Data available at the Library of Congress.

ISBN: 978-1-60887-303-6

ROOTS of PEACE   🌳 REPLANTED PAPER

Insight Editions, in association with Roots of Peace, will plant two trees for each tree used in the manufacturing of this book. Roots of Peace is an internationally renowned humanitarian organization dedicated to eradicating land mines worldwide and converting war-torn lands into productive farms and wildlife habitats. Roots of Peace will plant two million fruit and nut trees in Afghanistan and provide farmers there with the skills and support necessary for sustainable land use.

Manufactured in China

10 9 8 7 6 5 4 3 2 1